THE BLESSED HOPE

Heaven Is Coming To Earth

BY
PAUL & NUALA O'HIGGINS

THE BLESSED HOPE

THE BLESSED HOPE
Heaven Is Coming To Earth
By Paul & Nuala O'Higgins

Published© 2014 By Reconciliation Outreach
ISBN-13:978-1500696863
ISBN-10: 1500696862

Your book has been assigned a CreateSpace ISBN.

THE BLESSED HOPE

INTRODUCTION

JESUS WILL RETURN AS HE PROMISED

In the following pages we will look at some of the most important Biblical revelations concerning The End Times And The Return Of The Lord. There is much confusion on this subject but the scriptures say that God does not want us ignorant of these matters. Because of some highly speculative teaching, God's people have been left in confusion concerning one of the most important and comforting aspects of our faith: the Blessed Hope and the Return of The Lord.

In these pages we present the end time passages as understandable and as messages of
- Great hope
- exhortations to holiness
- and freedom from the agenda of this present age

When Jesus was returning to Heaven from the Mount of Olives He spoke about His return.

THE BLESSED HOPE

"It is not for you to know times or seasons that the Father has fixed by his own authority. But you will receive power when the Holy Spirit has come upon you, and you will be my witnesses in Jerusalem and in all Judea and Samaria, and to the end of the earth." (Ac. 1:7-8)

The subject of end times should be approached neither with agnosticism on the one hand nor with arrogance on the other hand. We do not know everything about what the future holds, but neither has God left us in the dark about the future. There are many things that we do know already but there are many things that are not for us to know at this time, as God has chosen to keep them hidden until it is time for us to know them. Because many have speculated without real revelation about the interpretation of certain Bible passages they have forced the scriptures to say things that they do not say and have left a residue of confusion in the Body of Christ.

The end time scenario is like a JIGSAW. God has given us many of the most significant pieces but not the whole picture. God has given us enough information

> • to situate our lives against the backdrop of His plan

- to warn us about the vanity of this present age and
- to be filled with Hope concerning His future plans for world redemption.

The hope of Jesus' return is "THE BLESSED HOPE" of the believer. It is not "THE BLESSED DREAD." *"Waiting for our blessed hope, the appearing of the glory of our great God and Savior Jesus Christ"* (Titus 2:13)

When Jesus returns, He will establish His kingdom over the whole world and will remove the rule of darkness, ignorance and sin, that oppresses the earth today.. HEAVEN IS COMING TOWARDS EARTH. The earth will be under new management – the management of King Jesus.

"They shall not hurt or destroy in all my holy mountain; for the earth shall be full of the knowledge of the Lord as the waters cover the sea." (Isa 11:9)

No human ideology offers the hope that Jesus gives. His plan is sure! "And when he had said these things, as they were looking on, He was lifted up, and a cloud took And while they were gazing into heaven as he went, behold, two men stood by them in white robes, and said, "Men of Galilee, why do you stand looking into heaven? This Jesus, who was taken up from you into heaven, will come in the same way as you saw him go into heaven." (Acts 1:8)

JIGSAW PIECE I

THERE WILL BE A NEW HEAVENS AND A NEW EARTH

We understand the new heavens and the new earth to mean that the spiritual atmosphere over the earth and on the earth will be totally changed and made new. The demonic forces that rule in the heavenly places and on earth (according to Paul in Ephesians 6:12) will be deposed at the Lord's return. There will be a new heavens and a new earth. What a day that will be!

"But the heavens and the earth which are now preserved by the same word, are reserved for fire until the Day of Judgment and perdition of ungodly men. But, beloved, do not forget this one thing, that with the Lord one day is as a thousand years, and a thousand years as one day. The Lord is not slack concerning His promise, as some count slackness, but is longsuffering toward us, not willing that any should perish but that all should come to repentance But the day of the Lord will come as a thief in the night, in which the heavens will

pass away with a great noise, and the elements will melt with fervent heat; both the earth and the works that are in it will be burned up. Therefore, since all these things will be dissolved, what manner of persons ought you to be in holy conduct and godliness, looking for and hastening the coming of the day of God, because of which the heavens will be dissolved, being on fire, and the elements will melt with fervent heat? Nevertheless we, according to His promise, look for new heavens and a new earth in which righteousness dwells." (2 Pt. 3:7 -13)

The present earth is oppressed by the presence of demonic forces that operate in the heavens above us and on the earth.

"For we do not wrestle against flesh and blood, but

     (i)   *Against the rulers*
     (ii)   *Against the authorities,*
     (iii)   *Against the cosmic powers*
            over this present darkness,
     (iv)   *Against the spiritual forces of evil*
            in the heavenly places." (Eph 6:12)

The demons ("cosmic powers over this present darkness and spiritual forces of evil") that operate in the second heavens will be removed and the heavens will be cleansed and made new. Also the demonic rulers (forces) and authorities (powers) that operate on the earth to oppress us will be finally removed from the earth allowing the earth to be made new. Thus we will have a new heavens and a new earth. The socio-political order, now dominated by anti-Christ forces will be cleansed and the earth will be filled with the benign, loving wise. kindly rule of Jesus and His followers. This will be the Messianic Kingdom. God's New World Order will replace man's New World Order.

"It shall come to pass in the latter days that the mountain of the house of the Lord shall be established as the highest of the mountains, and shall be lifted up above the hills; and all the nations shall flow to it, and many peoples shall come, and say: "Come, let us go up to the mountain of the Lord, to the house of the God of Jacob, he will teach us his ways and we will walk in his paths." For out of Zion shall go the law, and the word of the Lord from Jerusalem. He shall judge between the nations, and shall decide disputes for many peoples; and they shall beat their swords into plowshares, and their spears into pruning hooks; nation shall not lift up sword against nation, neither shall they learn war anymore." (Isa. 2:2-4)

JIGSAW PIECE II

WILL THE EARTH BE DESTROYED?

"But the day of the Lord will come as a thief in the night, in which the heavens will pass away with a great noise, and the elements will melt with fervent heat; both the earth and the works that are in it will be burned up." (2 Peter 3:8)

There are some that teach that the earth will be totally destroyed and that God will then create a new heavens and a new earth with no relationship to the existing world. This explanation is not accurate as it takes Peter's statement out of context from Paul's' teaching in Romans Chapter 8 which states that the creation is to be redeemed not destroyed.

"For the creation was subjected to futility, not willingly, but because of him who subjected it, in hope, that the creation itself will be set free from its bondage to corruption and obtain the freedom of the glory of the children of God." (Rom 8: 20 - 23)

Peter does say *"the elements will melt"* and this seems to imply a complete destruction of the planet. However, the word 'elements' here is the Greek word 'stoichieon' means the elementary systems and principles that control the earth. It is not the same as the modern word 'element' used in chemistry. Paul uses the same word in Galatians 4:3,9 where he tells his readers not to be enslaved to the "elementary principles of the world" and urges them not return to worthless "elementary principles of the world.' Clearly he is not talking about physical elements but the enslaving systems of this present world order that operate in political, religious and economic systems. Peter therefore is not talking about the 'melting' of the physical elements. He is predicting the dissolution of the present world order. i.e. the present SYSTEMS that control and oppress the earth will melt and be replaced by the rule of Jesus.

There will be new political systems, economic systems, education systems, healthcare systems, cultural systems that will all be in perfect harmony with God' order. This will be the Kingdom of God. Peter's words are exactly in line with what David says in Psalm 68:1-2:

"God shall arise, his enemies shall be scattered; and those who hate him shall flee

before him! As smoke is driven away, so you shall drive them away; as wax melts before fire, so the wicked shall perish before God! But the righteous shall be glad; they shall exult before God; they shall be jubilant with joy!"

The present demonically manipulated world systems that have oppressed he earth will be replaced the Lord's appearing! In that day "the mountain of the house of the Lord shall be established as the highest of the mountains" (Isaiah 2:2)

What a day that will be!

JIGSAW PIECE III

OUR BODIES WILL BE TRANSFORMED

When the Lord comes our lowly bodies will be transformed - He will also complete His redemptive work in us. Our mortal bodies will put on immortality. The earth will be filled with the knowledge of the Lord and will be redeemed from its bondage to decay.

"For we know that the whole creation has been groaning together in the pains of childbirth until now. And not only the creation, but we ourselves, who have the first fruits of the Spirit, groan inwardly as we wait eagerly for adoption as sons, the redemption of our bodies." (Romans 8: 22 - 23)

"But our citizenship is in heaven, and from it we await a Savior, the Lord Jesus Christ, who will transform our lowly body to be like His glorious body, by the power that enables him even to subject all things to himself." (Philippians 3:20-21)

11

"Then comes the end, when He delivers the kingdom to God the Father after destroying every rule and every authority and power. For He must reign until he has put all his enemies under his feet. The last enemy to be destroyed is death. For "God has put all things in subjection under his feet." (1 Corinthians 15:27)

The last enemy to be destroyed is death. When He comes Jesus will destroy and remove the systems and strongholds that are opposed to the benign and loving will of God. This will create as we have seen a new heavens an a new earth. Death is not destroyed until Jesus comes and defeats every other rule.

JIGSAW PIECE IV

PAUL TEACHES ON THE COMING OF THE LORD

2 Thessalonians And In 1 Corinthians

"But we do not want you to be ignorant, brothers, about those who are asleep, that you may not grieve, as others do who have no hope. For since we believe that Jesus died and rose again, even so, through Jesus, God will bring with him those who have fallen asleep. For this we declare to you by a word from the Lord, that we who are alive, who are left until the coming of the Lord, will not precede those who have fallen asleep. For the Lord himself will descend from heaven with a cry of command, with the voice of an archangel, and with the sound of the trumpet of God. And the dead in Christ will rise first. Then we who are alive, who are left, will be caught up together with them in the clouds to meet the Lord in the air, and so we will always be with the Lord. Therefore encourage one another with these words." (2 Thess. 4:13-17)

THE BLESSED HOPE

"Behold! I tell you a mystery. We shall not all sleep, but we shall all be changed, in a moment, in the twinkling of an eye, at the last trumpet. For the trumpet will sound, and the dead will be raised imperishable, and we shall be changed. For this perishable body must put on the imperishable, and this mortal body must put on immortality. When the perishable puts on the imperishable, and the mortal puts on immortality, then shall come to pass the saying that is written: "Death is swallowed up in victory. "O death, where is your victory? O death, where is your sting?" (1 Cor. 15:51-55)

From these two passages in Paul's letters we learn the following and more.
Paul does not want us to be ignorant of
   (1) The fact that the Lord is Returning
   (2) That the believers who have gone on before us will come back with the Lord
   (3) That there will be no rising to meet the Lord in air UNTIL the return of the Lord with the believers who have gone before.
   (4) The believers who are alive on the earth will not rise to meet the Lord before the dead are raised. Because the dead in Christ will rise BEFORE the saints on the earth
   (5) At The Last Trumpet the dead will rise and receive new bodies Those who are alive and remaining at the return of The

14

Lord will receive redeemed bodies, and overcome the last enemy – death

(6) The coming of the Lord will be accompanied with the blast of a trumpet . This is The Last Trumpet.

Some have taught (erroneously) that the believers will rise in the resurrection before the coming of the Lord or before The Last Trumpet. Paul specifically says that Jesus will not return until The Last Trumpet (1 Cor. 15:51). Also the Book of Revelation reveals that the Lord will not return until the plagues on the earth are over (Rev 11:15). He will come and possess His Kingdom when the seventh trumpet (which is The Last Trumpet) is blown after all the plagues on the earth are finished and not before then. It is then the Lord will return to rule on the earth.

"Then the seventh angel blew his trumpet, (the last of seven) and there were loud voices in heaven, saying, "The kingdom of the world has become the kingdom of our Lord and of his Christ, and he shall reign forever and ever." (Revelation 11:15)

Paul is concerned that the believers should not be ignorant (as much of the church is today) that there will be no rising to meet to he Lord in the air

    (1)   Until the Lord returns to rule upon the earth

    (2)   Until the Last Trumpet.

This was the standard teaching of Christianity until the 19th century.

    The Book Of Revelation describes some of the plagues on the earth as the Trumpets are blown from heaven. When each of these trumpets is blown there is a further wave of trouble on the earth. Finally Revelation tells us that when the Last Trumpet is blown the mystery is ended and the Lord's rule is established. This coincides with Paul's statement that we will not receive resurrected bodies until the Last trump. (Rev. Chs. 8-11)

    "Then the seventh angel blew his trumpet, and there were loud voices in heaven, saying, *"The kingdom of the world has become the kingdom of our Lord and of his Christ, and he shall reign forever and ever."* (Revelation 11:15)   *"Behold! I tell you a mystery. We shall not all sleep, but we shall all be changed, in a moment, in the twinkling of an eye, at the last trumpet. For the trumpet will sound, and the dead will be raised imperishable, and we shall be changed."* (1 Corinthians 15:51-52)

THE BLESSED HOPE

The Bible assures us that God will not allow the earth to continue to be a place of turmoil, war and oppression forever. He will send Jesus back to establish His rule and reign on the earth. When this happens He will replace every other rule and authority with His own benign rule of healing, truth, righteousness, mercy and love. We will all walk in love and serve Him and serve one another.

"Everyone helps his neighbor and says to his brother, "Be of good courage" (Isaiah 41:6)

JIGSAW PIECE V

WILL THE CHURCH BE "RAPTURED" BEFORE JESUS RETURNS?

There is much popular but false teaching today that says the church will be removed from the earth before the Lord comes back to rule on the earth. It is astonishing to us that this teaching should be so widely accepted when it is clearly contradicted by the scriptures themselves which (as we have seen above) teach that the Lord does not come until the last trump and that the believers on earth do not rise before the saints who have gone on. This has become an unquestioned TRADITION in many parts of the evangelical church today. But it is only a tradition and is not supported by scripture. In fact the scripture specifically contradicts it.

This tradition is based on a false teaching that the last week of Daniels 70 week (490-year) prophecy has not yet been fulfilled. (Daniel 9:24-27) A Chilean Jesuit priest, Manuel Lacunza, who had been exiled to Europe in the last part of the 18th century, developed this teaching. In 1790 Lacunza published a three-volume book "The Coming of the Messiah in Glory and Majesty". In this book he (heretically) taught that the 70 week prophecy of Daniel 9 was about the Anti Christ instead of the true Christ. He also put forward the notion the last 7 years of Daniel's prophecy would be fulfilled at the end of the age when a vicious dictator (The Antichrist) would enter into a peace treaty with Israel. (See "Appendix I – Daniel's 70 Weeks")

The renowned Bible teacher, J.N. Darby of the Brethren movement, picked up this teaching and developed it further. Darby passed the teaching on to C. I. Scofield and it became a part of evangelical orthodoxy and tradition. It has become entrenched in many American evangelical Bible schools, Bible colleges and study Bibles notes up to this day. It has been popularized today by many TV ministries and by Tim Lahaye in the "Left Behind' series of books.

As well as grossly misrepresenting the prophecy of Daniel Chapter 9 about the death of Messiah and the covenant the Messiah makes, it teaches that the church will disappear from the earth before the Lord returns to the earth to rule.

THE BLESSED HOPE

It implies that there are two comings of the Lord

- 1st coming in Secret for the believer to escape tribulation
- 2nd coming publicly to establish His rule on the earth.

JIGSAW PIECE VI

WE WILL "MEET" THE LORD
IN THE AIR

"For this we declare to you by a word from the Lord, that we who are alive, who are left until the coming of the Lord, will not precede those who have fallen asleep. For the Lord himself will descend from heaven with a cry of command, with the voice of an archangel, and with the sound of the trumpet of God. And the dead in Christ will rise first. Then we who are alive, who are left, will be caught up together with them in the clouds to meet the Lord in the air, and so we will always be with the Lord." (1 Thess. 4:15-17)

Paul says that we will "MEET" the Lord in the air. What does it means to 'meet' the Lord? The word "meet' used here is the Greek word "apantesis". This word occurs only three times in the New Testament and the meaning is the same each time.

1) It is first used in the parable of the ten virgins, in which they are told, "Behold, the bridegroom! Come out to meet him" (Matt. 25:6). The bridegroom has been gone, and, as they see him returning, they run out to meet and welcome Him.

2) The second time this word is used is when Paul is on his way to Rome, and the disciples in the city went out to Three Inns "to meet" him. Once again, he is on his way to Rome and they go out to meet him to welcome him to Rome.

3) The final use of this word is in the "rapture" passage, in which the Lord is descending from heaven and we are caught up "to meet" Him. He is already coming down when we are caught up to welcome Him back exactly as in the parable of the wise virgins coming to meet the Bridegroom. We are caught up to welcome our Lord back to rule and reign on earth. In fact, this is the reason for the "rapture".

The word was used to describe what happens when a city would go to meet a retuning general coming back in triumph. It is exactly in this way that we will rise to meet Jesus in the air and welcome Him back to the planet as Messiah - King of Kings.

The ancient expression for the civic welcome of an important visitor or the triumphal entry of a new ruler into the capital city and thus to his reign is applied to Christ. "Then we who are alive, who are left, shall be caught up together with them in the clouds to meet the Lord (eis apantesin tou Kyriou) in the air; and so we shall always be with the Lord." The same thoughts occur in the parable of the ten virgins. The virgins leave to meet the bridegroom (eis apantesin tou nymphiou) i.e. the Lord, to whom they wish to give a festive reception (Matt. 25:1) (New International Dictionary)

People often ask, "Do you believe in "The Rapture'?" We say, "Yes. We do believe that we will rise to meet Him in the air AT His coming but not BEFORE His coming." We will not rise to meet before He comes to rule on the earth, but we will rise to meet Him when He comes. The Bible never uses the word "rapture", but it does speak about our rising to meet Him in the air.

JIGSAW PIECE VII

WHAT ABOUT THE TRIBULATION?

Jesus warned us that we, His followers, would have tribulation and difficulties in this world, But we should fear not as He has overcome the world. Christians in this present age are in a unique position. We are directly related to the throne of God and therefore in His care. We are no longer under the curse and therefore we are blessed. Nevertheless we live in a fallen world and a dangerous environment. This causes pressure and tribulation, injustice and persecution. We are not immune from persecution but God makes persecution work for our good and can supply our every need even in times of persecution. We should not be afraid of persecution or tribulation because God redeems it and makes it work for our good. Instead we should rejoice in it. *"In the world you will have tribulation. Be of good cheer; I have overcome the world."* (John 16:33)

When the Lord returns there will be no more tribulation.... but not until then. Because much persecution has come through the political realm, Christians often try to control the political order for their own survival and protection. These efforts can be commendable, and some may be called to this arena. However, no matter how great the Christian influence in society we will be unable to avoid tribulation, persecution and injustice until the Lord returns. The tribulations that believers experience do not destroy us but only work for our good as they conform us more to the image and likeness of Jesus.

"And we know that for those who love God all things work together for good. .... For I am sure that neither death nor life, nor angels nor rulers, nor things present nor things to come, nor powers, nor height nor depth, nor anything else in all creation, will be able to separate us from the love of God in Christ Jesus our Lord." (Rom. 8:28; 37-39)

When we become too preoccupied with the political order and with self-preservation we lose sight of the throne of God from where our life, provision and protection comes.

SEVEN-YEAR TRIBULATION?

The idea of a SEVEN-YEAR TRIBULATION comes from erroneous teaching that the final seven years of Daniel's 490-year prophecy have not already been fulfilled and will be fulfilled when a vicious dictator takes over the world just before the Lord returns. (See Appendix 1) It is speculated that he will seem to be a good dictator for the first part of the seven years of his reign but that the last three-and-a-half years of his reign will be vicious.

To preserve the believers from these last vicious days many Bible teachers speculate and falsely teach (because of wrong interpretation of scripture) that the Lord will return before these events to rapture the church.

The time of tribulation that Jesus spoke about is neither a seven-year period nor a three-and-a-half year period but is the entire era of Christian history. THE GREAT TRIBULATION is the whole time between Jesus' Ascension and Return. We are in The Great Tribulation right now in the earth. When we read church history we can see that the last 2000 years have been years of tribulation. When we read today's newspapers you will see that we still live in a world of great tribulation. We recommend "The Voice Of The Martyrs' Magazine and web site to those who have doubts that we are in tribulation today. (http://www.persecution.com) The church has been in tribulation since the beginning and will be until the end because no matter how great the influence and favor we have, we are not of this world.

The idea of being 'raptured' away from the end-time tribulations is almost unknown in the places where the church is being perecuted today. The idea of escape of tribulation has programmed many in the western church to believe that they can avoid persecution and trouble in this life on earth. The New Testament teaches

- That in the world you will have tribulation, but we are not to fear as He has overcome world. *"In the world you will have tribulation. But take heart; I have overcome the world."* (John 16:33)
- That we are to overcome as He overcame. (Rev. 3:21)
- that the present world order is not our home and that *"friendship with the world is enmity with God."* (James 4:4)

"Jesus answered, "My kingdom is not of this world. If my kingdom were of this world, my servants would have been fighting, that I might not be delivered over to the Jews. But my kingdom is not from the world." (John 18:33)

"Do you not know that friendship with the world is enmity with God? Therefore whoever wishes to be a friend of the world makes himself an enemy of God." (James 4:4)

"Through many tribulations we must enter

the kingdom of God." (Acts 14:22)

No matter how difficult life may be in the world God will never "leave nor forsake us" and we always need to have our eyes fixed on Him.

"Keep your life free from love of money, and be content with what you have, for he has said, "I will never leave you nor forsake you." So we can confidently say," The Lord is my helper; I will not fear; what can man do to me?" I will never leave you nor forsake you." (Hebr. 13:5-6)

"I am with you always, to the end of the age." (Matthew 28:20)

A concept that ignores the reality of tribulation (even as we live in the blessings of God's kingdom) has resulted in a mind-set that makes us compromise with the world. It has resulted in much worldliness among Christians.

"Beloved, we are God's children now, and what we will be has not yet appeared; but we know that when he appears_we shall be like him, because we shall see him as he is. 3 And everyone who thus hopes in him purifies himself as he is pure." (I John 3:2-3)

JIGSAW PIECE VIII

MAN OF SIN, & THE "FALLING AWAY"

"Now concerning the coming of our Lord Jesus Christ and our being gathered together to him ... Let no one deceive you in any way. For that day will not come, unless the falling away (departure) comes first, and the MAN OF SIN is revealed, the son of destruction, who opposes and exalts himself against every so-called god or object of worship, so that he takes his seat in the temple of God, proclaiming himself to be God. .. The coming of the lawless one is by the activity of Satan with all power and false signs and wonders, and with all wicked deception for those who are perishing, because they refused to love the truth and so be saved." (2 Thess. 1-4,9)

This passage has been the source of much speculation about who is "the man of sin" and when he will appear on the scene. Because the letter to the Thessalonians was written around 52 AD (about 18 years before the Fall of

Jerusalem) it is likely that this passage is about the Fall of Jerusalem in 70AD. Paul may have been reminding his readers of Jesus' teaching in Luke 21, that before His return Jerusalem will fall, the Temple be laid waste and the people scattered. He may be urging the Thessalonians not to be carried away with teaching that the return of the Lord could happen any day.

The return of the Lord will not happen before "THE MAN OF SIN" takes over the Temple and scatters the Jewish people – the departure. The phrase 'falling away' used in this passage can equally be translated as 'departure'. (It was translated in this way by pre King James translations.) In this case Paul was probably referring to the future (70AD) exile or 'departure' of the Jewish people from their land as Jesus and the prophets had predicted.

It is reasonable to conclude that the events of 70AD when the Roman general Titus Flavius captured Jerusalem and destroyed the Temple fulfilled this prophecy. Titus Flavius later became Emperor Titus and proclaimed himself to be a god (exactly as Paul predicted in the above passage).

ANTICHRIST & HUMANISM

In his letter to Timothy, Paul speaks about "the man of God" "that the man of God may be competent, equipped for every good work." (2 Tim. 3:17). The "man of God" is a generic phrase that signifies "the godly man". In Thessalonians he speaks about "the man of sin". It is possible that this is also a generic phrase for "the ungodly man". The ungodly man, "man of sin" is man who has declared independence from God and ignores His standards. In today's world MAN has thrown off all moral restraint and value systems. He has made himself god deciding for himself what he may or may not do. A society based on this radical humanism is developing throughout the world today. We also see counterfeit signs and wonders operated by "New Age" adherents and followers of Satan. We need to be aware during these times that all miracles and supernatural phenomena are not necessarily of the Lord. Otherwise we too can be deceived.

It is possible that the systems, which emerge from this atheistic mind set, will converge to produce a major political leader opposed to God's plan's and ways - the final Antichrist

JIGSAW PIECE IX

ANTICHRIST, BEAST & FALSE PROPHET

ANTICHRIST & 'THE BEAST'

"Children, it is the last hour, and as you have heard that antichrist is coming, so now MANY ANTICHRISTS HAVE COME. Therefore we know that it is the last hour." (1 John 2.18)

John writes that there are many antichrists. There have been many antichrist figures in history – leaders such as Titus Flavius and Hitler who have set them self in opposition to God's people and God's plan.

The book of Revelation speaks about a "beast" coming against Israel at the end of the age with the nature of a Lion a Leopard and a Bear. From the Book of Daniel We know that 'a beast' is a symbol of a nation, or confederation of nations often headed up by an Antichrist figure.

__THE BLESSED HOPE__

"And I saw A BEAST RISING OUT OF THE SEA, with ten horns and seven heads, with ten diadems on its horns and blasphemous names on its heads. And the beast that I saw was like a leopard; its feet were like a bear's, and its mouth was like a lion's mouth. And to it the dragon gave his power and his throne and great authority." (Rev. 13:1-2)

The Beast that comes against Israel at the end of the age with the nature of the Lion, Bear and Leopard will have the characteristics of all the empires that came against Israel in the past. In Daniel 7:4-6[1]

- The Leopard was Alexander's empire, which is modern Turkey, Syria and Egypt, (Daniel 7:6)
- The Bear was the Medes and The Persians which is modern Iran (Daniel 7:5)
- The Lion was Babylon - modern Iraq. (Dan. 7:4)

If the Lion, Bear and Leopard in Revelation are the same as the Lion, Bear and Leopard in Daniel then the last "Beast" that comes against Israel is a confederation of Middle Eastern States. The final confederation of

[1] We are indebted to Ellis H Skolfield's book 'The False Prophet" for his excelent insifght into the nature of 'Teh Beast' in Revvelation and recommend this book

33

nations that come against Israel may well be led by another antichrist although the Bible does not specifically say so.

FALSE PROPHET

"And I saw, coming out of the mouth of the dragon and out of the mouth of the beast and out of the mouth of the false prophet, three unclean spirits like frogs. For they are demonic spirits, performing signs, who go abroad to the kings of the whole world, to assemble them for battle on the great day of God the Almighty. ("Behold, I am coming like a thief! Blessed is the one who stays awake, keeping his garments on, that he may not go about naked and be seen exposed!") And they assembled them at the place that in Hebrew is called Armageddon." (Rev 16:13-16)

The Book of Revelation speaks of a False Prophet inspired by the devil (the dragon), which stirs up the nations to go to war against Israel. (Rev. 16:13)   John writes that the Antichrist is the one who denies the Father and the Son, Jesus. *"Who is the liar but he who denies that Jesus is the Christ? This is the antichrist, he who denies the Father and the Son."* (1 John 2:22) This is the position of much of Islam, which says that "there is one God and He has no Son" and denies the atoning death of Jesus and the Fatherhood of God.

The False Prophet is the ideology that empowers the Beast. Islamic teaching unites the Middle Eastern nations against Israel today. It denies God's promises to Israel, and the Atoning work of Jesus. Fanatic Islam also teaches that in the last days Allah will raise up from the Muslim world a leader, "The 12th Iman, who will destroy the "lie" of Christianity and Jewish rule over Jerusalem. This anti-Semitic teaching, (though not embraced by all Moslems) will stir up hatred of Israel in the Middle East and throughout the world. It will result in an invasion of Israel that will be put down by the Lord at His return. (Zechariah 14:3-4)

Those who do not receive a love of the truth will be influenced by the false prophet to be anti Israel and anti Semitic. The end-time scriptures are given to us as a warning to keep ourselves from the mindsets and ways of the world and to remain faithful to God's kingdom, God's plans and God's ways.

JIGSAW PIECE X

THE LAST DAYS
& THE END OF THE AGE

The return of the Jewish people to their land and the return of Jerusalem to Jewish control are the two great signs that we are at The End Of The Age.

The disciples asked Jesus this question: *"Tell us, when will these things be, and what will be the sign of your coming and of the close of the age?"* (Matthew 24:3) Jesus answered by predicting Israel's future. He predicted the fall of the Temple, the conquest of the City by Gentiles, the scattering of the Jewish people and the eventual return of Jerusalem to Jewish control. (See Matthew 24, Mark 13, and in Luke 21.)

THE BLESSED HOPE

In summary Jesus says that He will NOT return in power UNTIL the following events take place:

(1)   Jerusalem will be taken by Gentile forces, (Luke 21:20)

(2)   The Temple will be destroyed (Matthew 24:2)

(3)   The Jewish people scattered the nations (Luke 21:24) and

(4)   The Jewish people will be ragathered and Jerusalem will come back under Jewish control. (Luke 21:24) The Gentiles will trample down Jerusalem UNTIL the times of the Gentile's are fulfilled. *"They will fall by the edge of the sword and be led captive among all nations, and Jerusalem will be trampled underfoot by the Gentiles, UNTIL the times of the Gentiles are fulfilled."* (Lk 21:24) [See Appendix 2]

NOTE: "UNTIL" means 'not forever,' so when Jesus says that Jerusalem will be under gentile control "until" the gentile time is fulfilled, He is telling us that gentile control of Jerusalem will eventually come to an end.

"TIMES OF THE GENTILES" means "the period of gentile domination of the city of

Jerusalem" Jerusalem remained under Gentile domination until 1967. [See Appendix 2]

Jesus is also telling us that when the time of the gentiles is fulfilled (i.e. when Jerusalem comes back under Jewish control) we shall be at the end of the age, because He his answering the question "what is will be the sign of your coming and of the end of the age?"(Matthew 24:3) Since Jerusalem is now under Jewish control we know we are at the end of the age and we are, therefore, the first generation ever that can intelligently hope for the Lord's return in our lifetime. When we see Jerusalem back under Jewish control we are to "look up for our redemption is near!" (Look 21:28

THE WORD "REDEMPTION" refers to the completion of our personal redemption (including the redemption of our bodies), the redemption of Israel from the oppression of its enemies and the redemption of the planet from corruption under systems that are demonically influenced and not submitted to God. These events are all part of our BLESSED HOPE and will take place at the return of the Lord. The end of the 'times of the Gentiles' i.e. the return of Jerusalem to Jewish control is the sign that the redemption is near. Since Jerusalem is now under Jewish control since 1967 we can say that we are the first generation of believers that can intelligently hope for the return of the

Lord and the redemption to take place in our lifetime.

Until Jesus returns the earth will continue to be a place convulsed by wars, natural disasters, war, political strife and persecution of Jews and Christians. (Matt. 24:6-7; Luke 24:11) Less than 40 years after Jesus spoke these words the Romans brutally captured Jerusalem, destroyed the Temple and scattered the Jewish people. In 1967 Jerusalem came back under Jewish control for the first time since the Roman Conquest. According to Jesus the return of Jerusalem to Jewish control is THE SIGN that we are in the end of the age i.e. the end part of the last days and the times that immediately precedes His return.

"The Latter Days" is the period between Jesus' Ascension and Return.

"The End Of The Age" is (according to Jesus) the period between the Return of Jerusalem to Jewish control and the Return of the Lord. Since Jerusalem retuned to Jewish control in 1967, we now know that the end of the age began in 1967. We are therefore the first generation of people to be living at the end of the age.

The end of the age is also "The Time Of The Harvest" (Matthew 13:39) Jesus says, "The harvest is the end of the age" i.e. the end of the age is the time of the harvest. We are therefore now living in The Latter Days, in The End Of The Age and in The Time Of The Harvest.

According to Daniel "the end of the age" will be characterized by a time of increasing travel and information. "But you, Daniel, shut up the words and seal the book, until the time of the end. Many shall run to and fro, and knowledge shall increase." (Daniel 12:4)

This is an amazing and precise description of this present time. It will also be a time of continuing political upheaval and geological disruption but it will be also characterized by a harvest of global evangelism (harvest). "And because lawlessness will be increased, the love of many will grow cold. But the one who endures to the end will be saved. And this gospel of the kingdom will be proclaimed throughout the whole world as a testimony to all nations, and then the end will come." (Matthew 24:12-14)

JIGSAW PIECE XI

Special Tribulations At
The End Of The Age

We have seen that the time of between the Ascension of the Lord and His return is the time of The Last Days but that there is also another period of history called THE END OF THE AGE. The end of the age is the last part of the Last Days and is the period between the return of Jerusalem to Jewish control(1967) and the return of the Lord.

The book of Revelation divides the time between the Ascension of Jesus and His return into SEVEN SEALS. The metaphor of seals comes from the fact that writings were contained in scrolls. Each scroll was sealed. The seven seals open seven scrolls of successive events of history. The first scroll is opened by the first seal, (Rev. 6:1) the second is opened by the second seal, (Rev. 6:3) the third is opened by the third seal (Rev. 6:5) etc. Each seal opens a different scroll or chapter of history. The seventh scroll is the last chapter of history before the return of the Lord.

Seventh Seal: The Last Chapter Of This Age[2]

The Book Of Revelation pays special attention to The Seventh Seal - the last chapter of history before the return of the Lord. This is the scroll opened by the seventh seal.

Though we have been in tribulation since the Ascension of Jesus there is *a special period of more intense tribulation* that is reserved for the end of the age - the period immediately before the return of the LORD. These tribulations are the events of the seventh seal. They are described in Revelation 6 and 16

The seventh scroll or seal is divided into SEVEN EVENTS THAT WILL TAKE PLACE AT THE END OF THE AGE. Each of these events is announced by the blowing of a trumpet. The last of these events is the Last Trumpet or Seventh Trumpet. It is at the Seventh Trumpet that Jesus will return in triumph to take possession of the kingdoms of the world. *'Then the seventh angel sounded: And*

---

[2] We are indebted to David P. Ebaugh author of "The Key To The Book Of Revelation" for his insights into the 'seals', 'bowls' and 'trumpets', and recommend his book.

there were loud voices in heaven, saying, "The kingdoms of this world have become the kingdoms of our Lord and of His Christ, and He shall reign forever and ever!" ' (Rev. 12:15)

The Book Of Revelation predicts the conditions that will prevail on the earth just before the return of the Lord - at the seventh seal. The seventh seal contains SEVEN TRUMPETS and SEVEN BOWLS OF JUDGMENT.

Each trumpet and judgment bowl within the seventh seal describes special tribulations and stressful conditions that will exist on the earth in the period between the restoration of Jerusalem to Jewish control and the return of the Lord i.e. between 1967 and the return of the Lord at a date, which no one knows. We are now in the period of the seventh seal (containing the seven trumpets and bowls) - the end of the age. By examining what The Book Of Revelation says about the events of the seventh seal we can easily see that it describes global events that match this present period of time. Indeed the events described in The Seventh Seal (with its seven trumpets and bowls) only fit our time.

To sum up
- The seventh seal describes seven events each announced by the blowing of a trumpet by an angel,
- The last or seventh trump is the return of the Lord.

The events of the seventh seal are described in Revelation Chapters 8 - 11 as SEVEN TRUMPETS as an angel blowing a trumpet precedes each event. The *same* events are described a second time in Revelation 16 as the SEVEN BOWLS OF JUDGMENT as an angel pouring out a bowl of judgment precedes each event. So at the end of the age we have
- Seven angels with trumpets warning of judgment and
- Seven angels with bowls bringing the judgments.

It is apparent that both Revelation chapters 8-11 and Revelation Chapter 16 are describing the same events - the events of the last chapter of history before the return of the Lord.

Seven Trumpets Announced

"When He opened the seventh seal, ... I saw the seven angels who stand before God, and to them were given seven trumpets." (Rev. 8:1)

Seven Angels With Bowls of Judgments

"Then I heard a loud voice from the temple saying to the seven angels, "Go and pour out the bowls of the wrath of God on the earth." (Rev 16:1)

First Trumpet: Vegetation Struck *"The first angel sounded: And hail and fire followed, mingled with blood, and they were thrown to the earth. And a third of the trees were burned up, and all green grass was burned up."* (Rev. 8:7)

First Judgment Bowl: Loathsome Sores (Rev 16:2)
"So the first went and poured out his bowl upon the earth, and a foul and loathsome sore came upon the men who had the mark of the beast and those who worshiped his image."

Second Trumpet: Seas Struck
"Then the second angel sounded: And something like a great mountain burning with fire was thrown into the sea, and a third of the sea became blood. And a third of the living creatures in the sea died, and a third of the ships were destroyed." (Rev. 8:8-9)

Second Judgment Bowl: The Sea Polluted
"Then the second angel poured out his bowl on the sea, and it became blood as of a dead man; & every living creature in the sea died." (Rev. 16:3)

Third Trumpet: The Waters Struck
"Then the third angel sounded: And a great star fell from heaven, burning like a torch, and it fell on a third of the rivers and on the

springs of water. The name of the star is Wormwood. A third of the waters became wormwood, and many men died from the water, because it was made bitter." (Rev. 8:10-11)

Third Judgment Bowl: Rivers Polluted

"Then the third angel poured out his bowl on the rivers and springs of water, and they became blood." (Rev 16:4-5)

Fourth Trumpet: The Heavens Struck

"Then the fourth angel sounded: And a third of the sun was struck, a third of the moon, and a third of the stars, so that a third of them were darkened. A third of the day did not shine, and likewise the night." (Rev. 8: 12-13)

Fourth Judgment Bowl: Sun Scorches

"Then the fourth angel poured out his bowl on the sun, and power was given to him to scorch men with fire." (Rev 16:8-9)

Fifth Trumpet: Locusts (Demons) Released From The Bottomless Pit

"Then the fifth angel sounded: And I saw a star fallen from heaven to the earth. To him was given the key to the bottomless pit. And he opened the bottomless pit,... and locusts came upon the earth. .. And they had as king over them the angel of the bottomless pit, whose name in Hebrew is Abaddon, but in Greek he has the name Apollyon." (Rev. 9:1-12)

Fifth Judgment Bowl: Darkness & Pain

"Then the fifth angel poured out his bowl on the throne of the beast, and his kingdom became full of darkness; and they gnawed their tongues because of the pain. They blasphemed the God of heaven because of their pains and their sores, and did not repent of their deeds." (Rev 16:10-11)

Sixth Trumpet: The Angels Release the From The Euphrates River

"Then the sixth angel sounded: And I heard a voice from the four horns of the golden altar which is before God, ... "Release the four angels who are bound at the great river Euphrates." So the four angels, who had been prepared for the hour and day and month and year, were released to kill a third of mankind. Now the number of the army of the horsemen was two hundred million; I heard the number of them." (Rev. 9:13-16)

Sixth Judgment Bowl: Euphrates Dried Up

"Then the sixth angel poured out his bowl on the great river Euphrates, and its water was dried up, so that the way of the kings from the east might be prepared. And I saw three unclean spirits like frogs coming out of the mouth of the dragon, out of the mouth of the beast, and out of the mouth of the false prophet. For they are spirits of demons, performing signs, which go out

THE BLESSED HOPE

to the kings of the earth and of the whole world, to gather them to the battle of that great day of God Almighty. And they gathered them together to the place called in Hebrew, Armageddon." (Rev 16:12-16)

Seventh The Return Of The Lord

"Then the seventh angel sounded: And there were loud voices in heaven, saying, "The kingdoms of this world have become the kingdoms of our Lord and of His Christ, and He shall reign forever and ever!" And the twenty-four elders who sat before God on their thrones fell on their faces and worshiped God, saying: "We give You thanks, O Lord God Almighty,.. Because You have taken Your great power and reign" (Rev. 11:15-16)

Seventh Bowl: The End & Return Of The Lord

God's work is finished and Babylon Falls "Then the seventh angel poured out his bowl into the air, and a loud voice came out of the temple of heaven, from the throne, saying, "It is done!" (Rev. 16:17) "And great Babylon was remembered before God, to give her the cup of the wine of the fierceness of His wrath." (Rev. 16:19)

Revelation 8, 9 & 11 Seven Angels With Trumpets	Revelation 16 Seven Angels With Bowls
1. Vegetation Struck	1. Earth Struck
2. Seas Struck	2. Seas Struck
3. Waters Struck	3. Waters Struck
4. Heavens Struck	4. Heavens Struck
5. Demons Released	5. Demons Released
6. Armies Cross Euphrates	6. Armies Cross Euphrates
7. Jesus Returns	7. Jesus Returns

By looking at the 'trumpets' and the 'bowls' together (side by side) we can see that the end of the age will be characterized by problems with

1.   diseases related to the damage of the vegetation;

2.   damage to the ocean;

3.   damage to seas and rivers,

4.   damage effecting the heat from the sun

5.   Problems arising from the release of demons of darkness from the bottomless pit.

6.   We also see that demonic powers will gather the nations from the region of the Euphrates to fight against Israel. This will culminate in a battle in the Plain of Megiddo and will be stopped by the Lord. All the best humanistic efforts of man will have failed to solve these great problems. At the heart of all these global problems is the problem of peace in The Middle East.

7.   The coming of the Lord will bring an end to the 6,000 years of man's mismanagement of the world and the restoration of God's management of the world when heaven and earth welcome into blissful harmony under the rule of Jesus the Heavenly Man.

We can easily see that the seventh seal describes life at the end of the twentieth century and the 21st century. The vegetation has been struck the seas and rivers have become polluted. The sun is warming the earth, legions of unclean demons have been released, and the powers of the Middle East are coming against Israel

6th Trumpet, 6th Bowl Of Judgment & Armageddon

Now let us look more closely at the sixth trumpet and sixth bowl of Judgment - the last events before the return of the Lord.   *"I   heard a loud voice from the four horns of the golden altar which is before God, ... "Release the four angels who are bound at the great river* **Euphrates.***" So the four angels, who had been prepared for the hour and day and month and year, were released to kill a third of mankind. Now the number of the army of the horsemen was two hundred million; I heard the number of them."* (Rev. 9:13-16)

"Then the sixth angel poured out his bowl on the great river **Euphrates,** *and its water was*

*dried up, so that the way of the kings from the east might be prepared. And I saw three unclean spirits like frogs coming out of the mouth of the **dragon**, out of the mouth of the **beast**, and out of the mouth of the **false prophet**. For they are spirits of demons, performing signs, which go out to the kings of the earth and of the whole world, to gather them to the battle of that great day of God Almighty. ...'And they gathered them together to the place called in Hebrew, **Armageddon.** "* (Rev. 16:12-16)

From these two passages we can see that, just before the return of the Lord, armies from the Euphrates region of the Middle East - the area of Modern Syria, Iraq and Iran will come against Israel to seek to destroy it.

Dragon, Beast & False Prophet

Revelation shows that the Middle Eastern powers that come against Israel will be brought together by

- **THE DRAGON**
- **THE FALSE PROPHET**
- **THE BEAST**

"And I saw three unclean spirits like frogs coming out of the mouth of the dragon, out of the mouth of the beast, and out of the mouth of the false prophet." (Rev. 16:13)

We know from Revelation 12:9 that **THE DRAGON IS THE DEVIL:** *"So the great dragon was cast out, that serpent of old, called* *the Devil and Satan, who deceives the whole world; he was cast to the earth, and his angels were cast out with him."*

We know that the spirit of true prophecy is that which testifies to Jesus and the Father. *"For the testimony of Jesus is the spirit of prophecy."* (Rev. 19:10) The false prophet is a false theology and preaching that opposes the testimony of Jesus as Savior, God as a loving Father.

The false prophet is the spirit, which opposes the revelation of God as love, God as Father, and opposes God's prophetic promises to Israel.

This exactly describe the spirit of fanatic Islam. The FALSE PROPHET (false ideology inspired by the Devil) prevails in anti-Israel, anti-Christian FANATIC JIHADIST ISLAM TODAY. It controls and oppresses many of the people of the Middle East. It is a demonic spirit characterized by undiluted hatred.

In Bible prophecy according to Daniel the term "BEAST" is used to describe a nation or a confederation of nations. (See Daniel Chapter 7)

The BEAST in Revelation 16 is the confederation of nations from the river Euphrates that is brought together by their shared demonically inspired ideology.) In their hatred of Israel and the God of the covenant these nations centered in the region of the Euphrates River will come against Israel.

So we can now clearly see what the sixth trumpet and sixth bowls are talking about. The devil, working through anti-Christian, anti-Israel propaganda, unites the political powers around the Euphrates River to come against Israel to destroy it. In his is hatred against the plan of God to restore Israel and unite mankind under the loving rule of God's Son, the devil unites political forces from the Euphrates area of the Middle East to hate Israel and Christians and to seek to destroy it. The devil works not directly by influencing people to hatred by means of an evil ideology, to come together politically against Israel

In the days of Nazi Germany we see that the devil worked through the false ideology of Nazism to unite several nations in a coalition to expand their power and seek to annihilate the people of Israel.

John sees that at the sixth trumpet & bowl, just before the Lord returns, the devil will work through some false ideology to incite the kings of the Euphrates river area to come against Israel.

The ideology that unites the Middle Eastern nations of The Euphrates area   is fanatic Jihadist Islam. This ideology is rising by force in this region and is intent on destroying Israel. They are politically united with anti-Israel and an anti Christian ideology that is inspired by the devil as Nazism was in the 20th Century.

Zechariah 14 seems to describe the same events as the events of the sixth trumpet and sixth bowl. When the nations who hate Israel come against it to destroy it. The Lord stops the war and comes in triumph to the Mount of Olives.

"Behold, the day of the Lord cometh, and thy spoil shall be divided in the midst of thee. For I will gather all nations against Jerusalem to battle; and the city shall be taken, and the houses rifled, and the women ravished; and half of the city shall go forth into captivity, and the residue of the people shall not be cut off from the city. Then the Lord will go forth and fight against those nations, as He fights in the day of battle. And in that day His feet will stand on the Mount of Olives, which faces Jerusalem on the east. And the Mount of Olives shall be split in two." (Zech. 14:1-4)

They will come against Israel and will only be defeated at Armageddon by the direct intervention by Israel's Messiah.

(Note God does not want us to use the Bible to hate Muslims or Arabs. God loves them and sent His Son to die for them also. What we see here is the defeat of a demonic ideology that has oppressed them and which seeks to destroy Israel.)

THE BLESSED HOPE

The Lord because He watches over His promises will not permit them to destroy Israel and will overthrow them by the word of His command at the valley of Armageddon in Central Israel. (Rev. 19:11-15; Zech. 14:4)

Paul's End-Time Events Compared With John's

We have seen that the sixth bowl and sixth seal describe the armies of the nations around the River Euphrates area of the middle East marching, in demonically inspired hatred, against Israel (Rev. 9:14; Rev. 16:12). God permits the restraining 'angels' to be removed and they advance on Israel where they are defeated by the Messiah Jesus as He returns in triumph. (Rev. 19:1; Rev. 19:11,15, 19-21)

"Now I saw heaven opened, and behold, a white horse. And He who sat on him was called Faithful and True, and in righteousness He judges and makes war. .... Now out of His mouth goes a sharp two edged sword[3], that with it He should strike the nations. And He Himself will rule them with a rod of iron. He Himself treads the winepress of the fierceness and wrath of

[3] Some commentators interpret the *'two edged sword'* in the Lord's mouth as literal but Hebrews 4:12 describes the word of God as a *"two-edged sword"* and we can reasonably assume the two edged sword in the Lord's mouth in Rev. 19 is His Word of authority and command and not a literal sword.

Almighty God. And He has on His robe and on His thigh a name written: King of Kings and Lord of Lords..... And I saw the beast, the kings of the earth, and their armies, gathered together to make war against Him who sat on the horse and against His army. Then the beast was captured, and with him the false prophet who worked signs in his presence, by which he deceived those who received the mark of the beast and those who worshiped his image. These two were cast alive into the lake of fire burning with brimstone. And the rest were killed with the sword which proceeded from the mouth of Him who sat on the horse. And all the birds were filled with their flesh."

When we compare these events with the events described in 2 Thessalonians 2:5-12 we can see a remarkable convergence. Is it possible that the sixth seal and sixth bowl of The Book of Revelation and 2 Thessalonians are describing the same events?

"Do you not remember that when I was still with you I told you these things? And now you know what is restraining, that he may be revealed in his own time. For the mystery of lawlessness is already at work; only he[4] (or it)

---

[4] The Greek word 'auton' is usually translated 'he' which impliyes an individual leader, but it could equally be translated 'it' referring

who now restrains will do so until he (or it) is taken out of the way. And then the lawless one will be revealed, whom the Lord will consume with the breath of His mouth and destroy with the brightness of His coming. The coming of the lawless one is according to the working of Satan, with all power, signs, and lying wonders, and with all unrighteous deception among those who perish, because they did not receive the love of the truth, that they might be saved. And for this reason God will send them strong delusion, that they should believe the lie, that they all may be condemned who did not believe the truth but had pleasure in unrighteousness." (2 Thess. 2:5-12)

Paul in 2 Thessalonians 2:5-12 sees
- an evil force (2 Thes. 5:8)
- raised up by the devil, (2 Thes. 5:9)
- being restrained at first (2 Thess. 5:7)
- then the restraint is removed (2 Th. 5:7)
- the evil continues its plot and is (2 Th. 5:8)
- defeated by the Lord at His return (2 Th. 5:8)
- by the breath of His mouth. (2 Th. 5:8)

John in Revelation Chapters 8, 9, 16 & 19) sees
- an evil force (the beast) (Rev. 16:12-14)

---

to a force such as an army or a movement. The Book of Revelation does not spek of an 'Antichrist' comiing agaisnt Israel but of a 'Beast coming against Israel.

- raised up by the devil/dragon (Rv.16:13)
- being released from restraint (Rev. 9:14)
- advancing against Israel (Rev. 16:16
- defeated by the Lord at His return (Rev. 19:11-21)
- by the two-edged sword from His mouth (the word of God) (Rev. 19:15)
- It seems that the Book of Revelation in Chapters 8, 9, 16 & 19 is depicts the exact same events as Paul depicts in 2 Thessalonians.

Paul also declares this demonically inspired force is raised up because people did not receive a love of the truth i.e. because they ignored the promises and admonitions of the word of God. (2 Thess. 5:12)

Armageddon & The Return Of The Lord

The Sixth Trumpet & Bowl describe the Battle of Armageddon and the Seventh Trumpet & Bowl describe the Lord's triumphant return. In the Book of Zechariah the last events before the return of the Lord is an effort to divide and destroy **Jerusalem**. In The Book of Revelation that last event before the return of the Lord is an effort to destroy **Israel**. The Book of Revelation's focus is on the survival of *Israel* and Zechariah's focus is on the survival of *Jerusalem*.

However, let's remember that The Battle of Armageddon and the tribulations of the seventh seal are not the focus of Biblical prophecy. They are the last troubles of the earth that precede the return of the Lord. The focus of prophecy is the faithfulness of God to His promise to redeem Israel and restore mankind and the whole creation to Gods' loving rule. The "BLESSED HOPE' that the earth and mankind will be released from man's mismanagement (represented by Babylon) and restored to God's perfect management under the leadership of Jesus the Messiah & king.

It appears that these events are going on today. The tribulations of the Seventh seal end with the destruction of the devil's anti-Israel anti Christian and hateful ideology. The Lord will reign and all the inhabitants of the earth will work under the rule of Jesus in the spirit of love to glorify God and serve each other. The birth pangs of tribulation are difficult now but the rend will be glorious.

The Lord will reign in glory from Jerusalem, the devil will be defeated and bound (Rev. 20:2) and we who are hoping in the Lord will experience the transformation of our lowly mortal bodies (Phil 3:21) and live with Him forever. *"So we shall we ever be with the Lord."* Let's prepare to meet the Bridegroom
WHAT A FUTURE! WHAT A HOPE!

THE BLESSED HOPE

JIG-SAW PIECE XII

THE DAVIDIC COVENANT

The Davidic Covenant is the fourth great covenant God made with Israel for the sake of all mankind. God solemnly promised David.

"When your days are fulfilled and you lie down with your fathers, I will raise up your offspring after you, who shall come forth from your body, and I will establish his kingdom. He shall build a house for my name, and I will establish the throne of his kingdom forever. I will be his Father, and he shall be my son... And your house and your kingdom shall be made sure forever before me, your throne shall be established forever." (2 Samuel 7:12-14,16)

"And it shall be, when your days are fulfilled, when you must go to be with your fathers, that I will set up your seed after you, who will be of your sons; and I will establish his kingdom. He shall build Me a house, and I will establish his throne forever. I will be his Father, and he shall be My son; and I will not take My mercy away from him, as I took it from him who was before you. And I will establish him in My house and in My kingdom forever; and his throne shall be established forever." (1 Chron.

17:11-14)

In Psalm 89 this promise is described as a covenant:

'I have exalted one chosen from the people
I have found my servant David;
with my holy oil I have anointed him, with
whom My hand shall be established...
My faithfulness and My Mercy shall be with
him....Also I will make him My first born, the
highest of the kings of the earth.
My mercy I will keep for him forever,
And My covenant shall stand firm with
His seed also I will make to endure forever, and
his throne as the days of heaven...
Once I have sworn by My holiness;
I will not lie to David
His seed shall endure forever,
And his throne as the sun before Me."
(Psalm 89:20-21; 24-29; 35-37)

Solomon & Jesus

Solomon (incorrectly) understood that these promises referred to himself and that the house that David's son would build was the Temple. Jesus however is greater than Solomon (Mt. 12:42) and His house is made not of physical stones but of living stones. His house is made of living stones and is built on Him the living Rock (Mt. 16:18; 1 Peter 2:5)

His temple is the body of people reconciled to God through His once-for-all sacrifice and filled with the spirit of eternal life, eternal love and eternal wisdom -The Holy Spirit. This temple is made up of Jew and Gentile made one in the Messiah from every tribe and tongue and people and nation in fulfillment with the promises God made with the Patriarchs of Israel. Unlike Solomon the one who fulfills David's Covenant will not be overcome by death and will reign forever.

"You will not leave my soul in Sheol, nor will You allow Your Holy One to see corruption." (Psalm 16:10)

God has sworn that this will happen. David's Son will sit on the throne of Israel. According to the prophets this promise would be fulfilled by one who was to be born in Bethlehem (Micah 5:2) and who would be called *"Mighty God."* (Isaiah 6:6)

"For unto us a Child is born, unto us a Son is given, and the government will be upon His shoulders. And His name will be called Wonderful, Counselor, Mighty God, Everlasting Father, and Prince of Peace. Of the increase of His government and peace there will be no end." (Is 9:6-7)

The one who will occupy the throne of David will also have victory over death, as His throne is everlasting and will not be passed on to successors.

As students of the scriptures we know that Jesus is the one who fulfills the Davidic

Covenant. The angel who spoke to Mary told her that her son *"will be great, and will be called the Son of the Most High; and the Lord will give to him the throne of his father David and he will reign over the house of Jacob forever; and of his kingdom there will be no end."* (Luke 1:32-33) In other words the Angel who came to Mary announced His coming as the one who was coming to fulfill the Davidic Covenant. She understood that she was to be the mother of the messiah who would occupy the throne of David forever.

Zechariah, the Father of John the Baptist also recognized that this son of Mary was promised one who would fulfill the promises of the Davidic Covenant. *"And his father Zacharias was filled with the Holy Ghost, and prophesied, saying, 'Blessed be the Lord God of Israel; for he has visited and redeemed his people, and has raised up an horn of salvation for us in the house of his servant David; as he spoke by the mouth of his holy prophets, who have been since the world began: that we should be saved from our enemies, and from the hand of all that hate us; to perform the mercy promised to our fathers, and to remember his holy covenant."* (Luke 1:68-72)

The complete fulfillment of David's Covenant is promised after the Jews have come back to the land of Israel and to Jerusalem. (See Isa. 2) We know from the scriptures that the nations will 'rage' against Israel and Jerusalem (Psalm 2). His return will fulfill the Davidic Covenant and bring peace from Jerusalem to Israel and the world.

"Now it shall come to pass in the last days that
the mountain of the Lord's house shall be
established on the top of the mountains, and
shall be exalted above the hills and all nations
shall flow to it.
Many people shall come and say:
'Come and let us go up to the mountain of the
Lord, to the house of the God of Jacob; He will
teach of His ways, and we shall walk in His
paths.'
For out of Zion shall go forth the law, and the
word of the Lord from Jerusalem.
He shall judge between the nations, and rebuke
many people;
They shall beat their swords into plowshares,
and their spears into pruning hooks.
Nation shall not lift up sword against nation,
Neither shall they learn war anymore." (Isaiah 2)

This covenant guarantees the restoration of Israel and the rule of the Messiah.

- The Abrahamic Covenant promises possession of the Land of Promise to Israel that will bless not jus them but all nations.
- The Sinai Covenant foreshadows the eternal sacrifice to bear the sins of the world, reveals God's righteous standards, man's unrighteousness and his need of

redemption and a new spirit.
- The New Covenant brings forgiveness and emancipation from sin through a suffering servant and the impartation of righteousness by God coming to dwell in us.
- The Davidic Covenant promises a triumphant glorious Ruler who brings in a world order under the rule of His righteousness and peace.

The present flow of history will climax in the triumphant coming (return) of the Messiah to fulfill the Davidic Covenant. This will be the culmination of all four covenants for Israel and the nations.

When Jesus came the first time He inaugurated the New Covenant and atoned for the sins of the world. Many of the Jewish people failed to recognize Him as the Messiah because He did not at that time fulfill all the promises contained in the Davidic Covenant and assert Himself as the triumphant heir to David's throne ruling from Jerusalem. This is the reason for His Second Coming. "This same Jesus who was taken up from you into heaven, will so come in like manner as you saw Him go into heaven." (Acts 1:10) He will return again to occupy the throne of David and to rule the earth from Jerusalem.

Then as the prophet foretold *"the earth will be filled with the knowledge of the glory of the Lord."* (Habakkuk 2:14)

"Now when you see these things begin to happen, look up, and lift up your heads for your redemption draws nigh." (Luke. 21:28)

The Davidic Covenant promises that the Messiah, son of David will reign on the throne of David forever. When Jesus came the first time He did not take His throne. He knew that the prophets had foretold a scattering of His people - the Jews- to the ends of the earth and a second destruction of the Temple. He also knew that His enthronement would not happen until the scattering and regathering of His people was completed.

As He was returning to the right hand of the Father His disciples asked him when he was about to restore the kingdom to Israel i.e. fulfill the Davidic Covenant.

*"Therefore, when they had come together, they asked Him, saying, "Lord, **will You at this time restore the kingdom to Israel?"** And He said to them, "It is not for you to know times or seasons which the Father has put in His own authority. But you shall receive power when the Holy Spirit has come upon you; and you shall be witnesses to Me in Jerusalem, and in all Judea and Samaria, and to the end of the earth.*

Now when He had spoken these things, while they watched, He was taken up, and a cloud received Him out of their sight. And while they looked steadfastly toward heaven as He *went up, behold, two men stood by them in white apparel, who also said, "Men of Galilee, why do you stand gazing up into heaven? **This same Jesus, who was taken up from you into heaven, will so come in like manner as you saw Him go into heaven.**"* (Acts 1: 6-11)

Jesus' unfinished business is to fulfill the Davidic Covenant and reign over Israel and over the whole world from Jerusalem. Heaven and earth will be united under His rule.

The gathering of the Jewish people to their land is an essential step and necessary condition for the return of the Lord to fulfill the Davidic covenant and take the throne of David as He promised.

This is the Blessed Hope

JIGSAW PIECE XIII

THREE GREAT MOVEMENTS
AT THE END OF THE AGE

As we have seen above in Daniel 12:4, the end of the age will be characterized as a time of global travel and of increase of knowledge. These are cultural and sociological phenomena. But what spiritual happenings will be taking place at the end of the age?

Three great movements from heaven will characterize the end of the age

(1) The Regathering Of Israel To Its Land

(2) The Preaching Of The Gospel To The Nations

(3) The Preparation Of The "Bride Of Christ"

(1)THE REGATHERING OF THE JEWISH TO ITS LAND (Luke 21:24; Ezekiel 36 & 37; Jeremiah 23:3: Isaiah 11:11; Amos 9:11)

"In that day the Lord will extend his hand yet a second time to recover the remnant that remains of his people, from Assyria, from Egypt, from Pathros, from Cush, from Elam, from Shinar, from Hamath, and from the coastlands

of the sea. He will raise a signal for the nations and will assemble the banished of Israel, and gather the dispersed of Judah <u>from the four corners of the earth</u>" (Isaiah 11:11)

"Then I will gather the remnant of my flock out <u>of all the nations</u> where I have driven them, and I will bring them back to their fold, and they shall be fruitful and multiply." (Jeremiah 23:3)

Notice in the above passages that the Lord has promised to bring Israel back from all the nations. The great prophets, from Moses to Jesus, foretold this regathering of the Jewish people from "all the nations". The regathering from Babylon was from only one nation but today's regathering is from *"all the nations"* and from *"the four corners of the earth."*

Many will recognize that it was the hand of the Lord that scattered Israel for her disobedience. But if we recognize His hand in their scattering we must also recognize it in their regathering. *"Hear the word of the Lord, O nations, and declare it in the coastlands far away; say, 'He who scattered Israel will gather him, and will keep him as a shepherd keeps his flock."* (Jeremiah 31:10)

(2) **THE GOING FORTH OF THE GOSPEL TO THE NATIONS (Matt. 24)**

"And this gospel of the kingdom will be proclaimed throughout the whole world as a testimony to all nations, and then the end will come." (Matthew 24:14)

Since the end of the age is the last part of the latter days we know for sure that during this period God will continue to pour out His Sprit on all flesh. *"And it shall come to pass in the latter days, that I will pour out my Spirit on all flesh your sons and your daughters shall prophesy your old men shall dream dreams and your young men shall see visions. Even on the male and female servant in those days I will pour out my Spirit."* (Joel 2:28-29)

Peter interpreted this passage as being fulfilled by outpouring of the Holy Spirit on all who call on the Lord (Acts 2). This has been going on since the Book of Acts.

In Acts 15 the apostles gathered to decide what to do with Gentile believers experiencing signs and wonders. James interprets this as the fulfillment of Amos 9 referring to Jew and Gentile together before the Ark at the Tabernacle of David. (Acts 15:16). In Amos 9 14-

15, the prophet speaking of today says: *"I will restore the fortunes of my people Israel, and they shall rebuild the ruined cities and inhabit them; they shall plant vineyards and drink their wine, and they shall make gardens and eat their fruit."* (Amos 9:11-15)

The vine was not grown in Israel during Turkish rule (1417-1917) but since the Jewish people have returned to their land it is once again flourishing. Here we see the Lord connecting together the regathering of Israel to the land, the preaching of the gospel with signs and wonders and the coming together of Jewish and Gentile believers in Him.

(3) THE PREPARATION OF "THE BRIDE."

The Spirit of God will be especially active at the end of the age to prepare the "Bride" to meet the "Bridegroom". The Bride is a metaphor for dedicated disciples who trust and obey Him and put all their hopes in Him and His plan for the earth. When Jesus returns He will not reign as a Monarch. He will reign with His companions, the Bride of Christ, The Overcomers, The Sons of God.

"Let us rejoice and exult and give him the

glory, for the marriage of the Lamb has come, and his Bride has made herself ready; I it was granted her to clothe herself with fine linen, bright and pure - for the fine linen is the righteous deeds of the saints." (Rev 19 - 7-8)

The Bride is in preparation now. She is "putting off" everything not pleasing to the Lord and "putting on" "the righteous deeds of the saints" which can only come from surrender to His righteousness within, and not from any religious activity. God is calling us to Himself to live in union with Him and to align our lives with Him and with His agenda. He wants us to be alert to the signs of the times like the 'wise virgins in the parable (Mt. 25). He calls us to set our "hope fully on the grace that will be brought to you at the revelation of Jesus Christ. (1 Peter 1:13) and to live fruitful lives in this world without being entangled in its ways or agenda.

The Book of Revelation uses two metaphors for those who will rule and reign with Jesus on His return, "The Bride of Christ" and "The Overcomers". While Chapter 19 speaks about the Bride of Christ, Chapters 2 & 3, speaks about The Overcomers. These chapters show us clearly that the Bride/Overcomers are not ones that escape tribulation but go through it without compromise or loss of faith. They learn to overcome evil with good and adversity with faith. *"And this is the victory that has overcome the world - our faith."* (1 John 5:4)

God uses the adversities of this world to purify His overcomers and to prepare them for Himself. He is coming for a *"Bride without spot or wrinkle"* - a people who will be like Him and who have overcome the pressures of the world, the flesh and the devil.

"He who overcomes, I will grant him to sit with me on my throne, as I also overcame and sat down with my Father on his throne." (Revelation 3:21)

"For the Lord disciplines the one he loves, and chastises every son whom he receives. It is for discipline that you have to endure. God is treating you as sons. For what son is there whom his father does not discipline? If you are left without discipline, in which all have participated, then you are illegitimate children and not sons. Besides this, we have had earthly fathers who disciplined us and we respected them. Shall we not much more be subject to the Father of spirits and live? For they disciplined us for a short time as it seemed best to them, but he disciplines us for our good, THAT WE MAY SHARE HIS HOLINESS. For the moment all

discipline seems painful rather than pleasant, but later it yields the peaceful fruit of righteousness to those who have been trained by it." (Hebrews 12:7-11)

The Bride will share His holiness.

JIGSAW PIECE XIV

WHAT'S NEXT FOR ISRAEL?

After Israel's return to their land, the Bible predicts

1. that Jerusalem will be a major problem to the surrounding nations. *"Behold, I am about to make Jerusalem a cup of staggering to all the surrounding peoples. The siege of Jerusalem will also be against Judah. On that day I will make Jerusalem a heavy stone for all the peoples. All who lift it will surely hurt themselves. And all the nations of the earth will gather against it."* (Zech. 12:2-3)

2. The Israeli people will recognize the saving work of Jesus. *"And I will pour out on the house of David and the inhabitants of Jerusalem a spirit of grace and supplication, so that, when they look on me, on him whom they have pierced, they shall mourn for him, as one mourns for an only child, and weep*

> *bitterly over him, as one weeps over a firstborn."* (Zechariah 12:10)

This pouring out on Israel of the grace of repentance also fulfills the prophetic words of the apostle Paul *"And even they, if they do not continue in their unbelief, will be grafted in, for God has the power to graft them in again. For if you were cut from what is by nature a wild olive tree, and grafted, contrary to nature, into a cultivated olive tree, how much more will these, the natural branches, be grafted back into their own olive tree. "Lest you be wise in your own sight, I want you to understand this mystery, brothers: a partial hardening has come upon Israel, until the fullness of the Gentiles has come in. And in this way all Israel will be saved, as it is written," The Deliverer will come from Zion, he will banish ungodliness from Jacob"; "and this will be my covenant with them when I take away their sins."* (Romans 11:23-27)

God will never forget Israel. Even though the majority of Israel has rejected the gospel in the past, God is about to pour out His spirit on them and they will recognize the work of the Messiah Jesus sand *"all Israel will be saved'*. They will experience a major revival and become a spirit filled nation. The effects of this great awakening of he Jewish people will shake the whole body of believers throughout the world and trigger worldwide revival. This great revival is already beginning to happen and should encourage us to be especially supportive of the Messianic movement in Israel with our prayers and with our love. *"For if their rejection means the reconciliation of the world, what will their acceptance mean but life from the dead?"* (Romans 11:15)

ELIJAH IS COMING

"Behold, I will send you Elijah the prophet before the great and awesome day of the Lord comes. And he will turn the hearts of fathers to their children and the hearts of children to their fathers, lest I come and strike the land with a decree of utter destruction." (Malachi 4:5)

"And His disciples asked Him, saying, "Why then do the scribes say that Elijah has to come first?" And Jesus answered them, "Elijah is indeed coming first, and shall restore all matters "But I say to you that Elijah has already come, and they did not recognize him but did to him whatever they wished. In this way the Son of Adam is also about to suffer by them. Then the disciples understood that He had spoken to them about John the Baptist." (Matthew 17:10-13)

Jesus recognized that John the Baptist had fulfilled this scripture when he called the nation to repentance and to recognize Jesus as the Lamb of God. Obviously He was not saying that John was the reincarnation of Elijah, but that he carried as similar anointing and ministry as Elijah.

He also indicates that there is a future fulfillment of this scripture. This does not mean that the prophet Elijah will be walking around Israel but that the spirit of repentance that was carried by Elijah and John the Baptist will be seen again in Israel again. Two factors are involved in this: national repentance and recognition of Jesus as the Lamb of God. This is exactly what Zechariah describes in Chapter 12 - as we have seen. Many nations will go to war against Jerusalem and try to divide it. Then The Lord will return to the Mount of Olives and establish His reign on the earth.

"Behold, the day is coming for the Lord, when the spoil taken from you will be divided in your midst. For I will gather all the nations against Jerusalem to battle, and the city shall be taken and the houses plundered and the women raped. Half of the city shall go out into exile, but the rest of the people shall not be cut off from the city. Then the Lord will go out and fight against those nations as when he fights on a day of battle. On that day his feet shall stand on the Mount of Olives that lies before Jerusalem on the east, and the Mount of Olives shall be split in

two from east to west by a very wide valley, so that one half of the Mount shall move northward, and the other half southward." (Zech. 14:1-4)

These prophecies from Zechariah certainly seem to be in the process of being fulfilled today. Jerusalem has become a major geopolitical problem. The surrounding Islamic nations are hostile to it and they are influencing the great powers (including the USA, Europe and Russia) to divide Jerusalem. Eventually this will lead to a war for Jerusalem. Zechariah predicts that the nations will succeed in dividing Jerusalem. When this happens the Lord will return to the Mount of Olives and establish His rule as we see in the prophecy of Zechariah 14 quoted above.

Though we are now (as we have seen) in the end of the Last Days - 'the end of the age', we do not know how long this period will last or 'the day or hour ' of His coming – but we say, "MARANATHA'

CONCLUSION

Many have projected their own meanings into end-time scriptures so that the true message of hope and comfort is often lost: Jesus is coming back, and the long era of human mismanagement of the planet will come to an end.

In the Book of Daniel we read, *"Go your way, Daniel, for the words are shut up and sealed until the time of the end."* (Daniel 12:9)

From our study of scripture we have seen we are living at a special period: "the time of the end" Scriptures that were once obscure are now becoming clear, and these prophecies are no longer "shut up and sealed." It is time for us to throw off merely traditional interpretations based on 18th and 19th century speculation.

We have not tried to interpret every scripture pertaining to the end times. We have, however, shown the scriptures shine amazing light into the purpose of God for world history, for Israel and for the believer. "Without a vision the people perish". With God's vision of His mighty plans revealed in His Word, we can live in hope. "And we have something more sure, the prophetic word, to which you will do well to pay attention as to a lamp shining in a dark place, until the day dawns and the morning star rises in your heart." (2 Peter 1:19)

Our awareness of the times should never distract us from our Christian walk. If these scriptures do not affect our WALK we have not touched their true message. The end time revelations are not given to puff us up with knowledge, but to encourage us to live whole-heartedly for God and for our Savior. They are not for our head but for our feet. They change our perspective from the trivial visions of this world and lift our vision to the High calling of God's amazing plan.

We are the Bride making ourselves ready for our King, by continually yielding to and drawing from His life in us. It is time, as never before, to walk in the Spirit and not in the flesh. "Do not love the world or the things in the world. If anyone loves the world, the love of the Father is not in him For all that is in the world the desires of the flesh and the desires of the eyes and pride in possessions is not from the Father but is from the world. And the world is passing away along with its desires, but whoever does the will of God abides forever." (1 John 2:16-17)

THE BLESSED HOPE

"For the powers of the heavens will be shaken. And then they will see the Son of Man coming in a cloud with power and great glory. Now when these things begin to take place, straighten up and raise your heads, because your redemption is drawing near." (Luke 21:28)

APPENDIX I

DANIEL'S 70 WEEKS

Daniel Chapter 9 contains the most amazing prophecy concerning the time of the coming of the Messiah. Various man-made interpretations have obscured the beauty and clarity of this awesome prophecy, which gives the exact date of the coming of the Messiah. This prophecy equals the suffering Servant Prophecy of Isaiah 53. It leaves no margin for dispute concerning the identity of the Messiah – Jesus. It predicts

- The date of his coming,
- His inauguration of the New Covenant,
- His death and
- The destruction of Jerusalem following His death.

Daniel was given a revelation of a 490-year period following a decree to rebuild Jerusalem. He predicted that in the last part of this 490-year period the Messiah would be killed and make a covenant.

Daniel calls the 490-year period "70 weeks" i.e. 70 periods of 7 years. This pattern of a day representing a year and seven days representing seven years is also found in Ezekiel 4:5.

Daniel divides the 70 weeks of years (490) into three sections

- The first seven weeks, i.e. the first 49 years – years 1 to 49
- The next sixty two weeks i.e. the next 434 years   (62 x 7) - years 50 to 483
- And the seventieth week (the last seven years) - years 484 to 490 .

(49 yrs. +434 yrs. +7 yrs. = 490 yrs.)

Daniel's 490 year time period begins from the decree to restore and rebuild Jerusalem.

The prophecy is recorded in Daniel chapter 9:24 – 27)

24* "Seventy weeks (weeks of years) are determined upon your people and upon your holy city,

- to finish the transgression,
- and to make an end of sins,
- and to make reconciliation for iniquity,
- and to bring in everlasting righteousness,
- and to seal up the vision and prophecy,
- and to anoint the most Holy (the Messiah)."

Paraphrase: The Messiah will

- come within 490 years of a certain decree to restore and rebuild Jerusalem)
- finish the transgression

- put an end to sin
- atone for wickedness
- bring in eternal righteousness.
- seal up vision and prophecy

25a "Know therefore and understand, that from the going forth of the commandment to restore and to build Jerusalem unto the Messiah the Prince shall be seven weeks, and sixty two weeks." (i.e. 69 weeks of years i.e. 69 x 7 = 483 years)
Paraphrase: The Messiah will come 483 years after a decree is issued to restore and rebuild Jerusalem.)

25b "the street shall be built again, and the wall, even in troublous times."
Paraphrase: Though Jerusalem will be rebuilt, it will know troubled times and not be in great prosperity.

26a "And after (the) sixty two weeks shall Messiah be cut off, but not for himself"
Paraphrase: Since the sixty-two weeks come after the first seven years, this means after 69 weeks of years i.e. after 483 (69 x7) years, the Messiah will be cut off on behalf of others. This is a reference to His sacrifice on our behalf.

26b "and the people of the prince that shall come shall destroy the city and the sanctuary; and the

end thereof shall be with a flood, and unto the end of the war desolations are determined."
Paraphrase: After the Messiah is cut off an invading prince will destroy Jerusalem and the Temple. (Within a generation After Jesus' death the Roman army conquered Jerusalem and destroyed the Temple)

27* "And he shall confirm the covenant with many for (during) one week: and in the midst of the week he shall cause the sacrifice and the oblation to cease, "
Paraphrase: In the middle of the last seven years of the 490-year period He (the Messiah) will make a covenant with many and put an end to sacrifice and offerings and the Temple Mount will become defiled until the end by the abomination of desolations. (Daniel 9:24-27) This is a clear prophecy of the New Covenant. In the inauguration of the New Covenant Jesus actually echoes these words: "This is my blood of the new covenant which is shed for MANY." (Mark 14;24)

27b "and on the wing of the Temple he will set up (or will be set up) an abomination that causes desolation until the end is decreed an poured out upon him (it)."
Paraphrase: After the cutting off (death of the Messiah) an abomination will be set up on a side of the Temple making it uninhabitable by Jews

and desolating the Temple area. This will remain until the end. The Dome of The Rock established Islamic worship on the Temple Mount since the 7th century and makes it impossible for the Temple to be restored. It is the abomination that makes the Temple area desolate.

The Time of counting of the 70 weeks (490 years) begins with a decree to restore and rebuild Jerusalem. In 454 King Artaxerxes I (474-433) issued a decree in the twentieth year of his reign (Nehemiah Chapter 2). 454 BC is therefore the year that the 490-year clock begins.

454 BC + 490 brings us to 36 AD.

(There is no zero A.D. - the year after I B.C. is 1 A.D.)

The last 7 years of the 490 cycle are from 29 to 36 A.D. Jesus was born 4 BC and was killed "cut off" AD 30, exactly in the last week as Daniel prophesied. His death was followed by the destruction of Jerusalem as both He and Daniel predicted.

Daniel's prophecy predicts:

• the rebuilding of Jerusalem and its second destruction
• the coming of the Messiah before its second destruction
• the Messiah making atonement for sin
• the Messiah's (1st) coming will not bring a

golden age for Jerusalem, but on the contrary, Jerusalem will suffer from the hands of imperial powers until the end of the age.
Something will be placed on a wing of the Temple Mount that will make it desolate (The Dome of the Rock has desolated (i.e. made unclean and worship impossible on the Temple Mount since 688 A.D. until today.)

WHICH DECREE

The time line according to Daniel commences with a decree to restore and build Jerusalem. The Bible records several decrees from the Persian Kings, which permitted Jewish return to their land..

Ezra & Nehemiah record 4 decrees by Mede & Persian Kings permitting Jewish exiles to return from Babylon
1) The first was issued by Cyrus in the year 536 BC is recorded in Ezra 1:1
2) The second was issued by Darius in the year 419 BC recorded in Ezra 4:24; 6-12
3) The third was issued by Artaxerxes in the year 458 BC is recorded in Ezra 7:7-28
4) Artaxerxes issued the fourth in the year 454 BC is recorded in Nehemiah 2:1-17

Decree #1 by Cyrus was a permit to build the Temple (Ezra Chapter 1)
Decree #2 by Darius was a permit to continue building the Temple

Decree #3 by Artaxerxes was a permit to continue building the Temple (Ezra chapter 7) Decree #4 by Artaxerxes in the year 454 to restore and build Jerusalem (Nehemiah 2:5)

Artaxerxes decree to rebuild Jerusalem was issued in 454 BC is the only one that is a permit to build the City of Jerusalem. the others all have to do with the rebuilding of the Temple. It is therefore from this decree that Daniel's 490-year period begins.

490 years after this decree in 454 BC takes us to 35 AD. The ministry of Jesus was approximately from 26- 30 AD. It took place in the last seven years of Daniel's 490 years Jesus was cut off (crucified) exactly as Daniel in the last seven years of the 490 years.

This view is supported by Julius Africanus - the late 2nd century historian who influenced Eusebius and early Christian writers. Many renowned chronologists such as Bishop Ussher, Walvrood, Dwight Pentecost, Unger and most present day bible chronologists agree with this interpretation of Daniel.

The Messiah was to be cut off and make a covenant after 69 periods of 7 years and before 70 periods of seven years; i.e. between 483 and 490 years after Artaxerxes decree.
454 BC + 483 = 29 AD
454 BC + 490 = 36 AD

Jesus died between 29 and 36 AD - exactly as Daniel predicted! The prophecy is not about the Antichrist, as many have falsely taught. It is about the true Messiah Jesus. It is not about a future event in history but about an event that has already taken place – the greatest event in history.

It is simply false teaching to say that Daniel's 490-year prophecy remains to be fulfilled in the future. Any end time theory based on the notion that this period is not fulfilled should be dismissed immediately .

CONCLUSION

This is one of the most amazing prophecies concerning the coming of the Messiah – Yeshua. He fulfilled it to the letter.

It explains
- the exact date of His crucifixion,
- that He would come to atone for our sins,
- bring a covenant (i.e. the New covenant);
- that He would die and
- that His death would be followed by a further desolation of Jerusalem and of the Temple Mount.

How sad that this great prophecy, which more than any other points to the identity of the real Messiah, and explains why the Messiah's coming did not bring in the glorious age has been obscured by the teaching of Lacunza,

THE BLESSED HOPE

Darby, Scofield etc.

The main objection that Jewish people have to the Messianic claim of Jesus is that He did not bring the glorious age. However, Daniel's prophecy clearly predicts that the Messiah's work would be followed by an invasion of the city and a period of desolation for the city.

APPENDIX II

ISRAEL'S EXILES PRECISELY
FORETOLD

Three times the children of Israel have been exiled from their land.
- 430 years in Egypt;
- 70 years in Babylon and
- 1900 years among the nations.

THE FIRST EXILE was foretold by Abraham and the exact time of the exile specified as 430 years (Genesis 15). Precisely on time, Israel came out of Egypt by the direct intervention of God to fulfill the word He had given to Abraham. In Genesis 15: 13-14 God says to Abraham: "Know for certain that your offspring will be sojourners in a land that is not theirs and will be servants there, and they will be afflicted for four hundred years. But I will bring judgment on the nation they serve, and afterward thy shall come out with great possessions." Here God predicts the events of the Exodus, when they came from Egypt with great possession. Here He also predicts the exact date of the Exodus – 400 years after Isaac is declared the heir.

In Exodus 12;40-41 we read "The sojourn of the people of Israel who lived in Egypt was 430 years. At the end of 430 years , on that very day, all the hosts of the Lord went out from the land of Egypt." The apparent discrepancy between the 400 years referred to in Genesis 15 and the 430 years referred to in Exodus 12 is easy to explain. The 400 years refers to the sojourn of the descendants of Abraham and begins from the year that Isaac was recognized as heir. The 430 years begins thirty years earlier when Abraham received the promise.

Had the children of Israel not left Egypt on the exact year then Abraham would have been a false prophet. Abraham had accurately heard from God - and God, who never lies - against all odds fulfilled His word.

Note: The children of Israel were not in Egypt for the entire 430 years, but were sojourners without inheritance for 430 years after the Land was promised to Abraham.

THE SECOND EXILE to the land of Babylon was a fulfillment of the prophetic words of Moses and Jeremiah. . Jeremiah specified the duration of the exile as 70 years (Jeremiah 29:10) and exactly as predicted God intervened again and returned Israel to its land. Their return was against all odds, including an attempt to annihilate and exterminate them in the days of Haman.

THE THIRD EXILE began with the fall of Jerusalem and the scattering of the Jewish people to the nations in 70 AD, and ended in the twentieth century when they came back to their land. Their regathering fulfills the prophesies of many of the great prophets including Moses, Isaiah, Ezekiel, Jeremiah, Hosea, Amos, Zechariah and Jesus. The climax of the modern return of Israel to their land is the establishment of the State of Israel in 1948 and the return of Jerusalem to their control in 1967. The regathering continues to this day .

DANIEL & JESUS PROPHECY ABOUT 1967

The key event in the present-day return is the restoration of Jerusalem to Jewish control. Amazingly the exact date for this was given by Jesus' interpretation of Daniel's prophecy in Daniel Chapter 8, which He referenced in Luke 21.24.

Daniel describes a vision of the conquest of the Middle East (including Jerusalem) by a King from Greece (Chapter 8:5 & Daniel 8:21). In the middle of the vision he asks the angel that brought him the message "For how long is the vision concerning the continual burnt offering, the transgression that makes desolate, and the giving over of the sanctuary and host to BE TRAMPLED UNDER FOOT?" (I.e. 'How long will Jerusalem be trampled underfoot?) The answer was given: "Unto evening and morning two thousand three hundred: and the sanctuary shall be cleansed." (Literal translation Daniel 8:13-14)

Daniel was told that Jerusalem (the place of the sanctuary) was to be under gentile domination for a 2,300 period. Most scholars agree this is a period of 2,300 years. It is commonly known that Alexander the Great of Greece conquered the Middle East in 334 BC. The prophecy indicates that Jerusalem will be "trampled underfoot by the Gentiles" for 2,300 hundred years from Alexander's conquest of the Middle East. This takes us, amazingly, to exactly 1967!! 334 BC +2300 =1967 AD. (Since there is no year 0 we add 1.)

There can be no doubt, therefore, that Jesus understood that Jerusalem would come back under Jewish sovereignty 2,300 years after Alexander's conquest i.e. 1967. When Jesus predicted the destruction of Jerusalem and the third exile of the Jewish people He quoted from the question that Daniel asked the angel, "How long is the vision of the sanctuary and host to be TRAMPLED UNDERFOOT?" (Daniel 8:14) and

He states simply that "Jerusalem will be TRAMPLED UNDERFOOT by the gentiles until the times of the gentiles are fulfilled." (Luke 21:24)

In the light of this tremendous prophecy of Daniel and its interpretation by Jesus there can be no doubt that June 1967 and the present day restoration of Jerusalem to Jewish control is the fulfillment of the divine plan and not a mere accident of history! Every Christian should know this - especially Bible teachers, politicians and journalists.

THE END OF THE AGE & PROPHECY
As we have seen through studying the prophecies concerning the restoration of Israel apart from speculation about the unfoldment of future days we can be certain that we are living at the end of the age .

Those who oppose the return of the Jewish people to their land are defying the plan and purposes of God. Not only that, but they are also declaring that the prophetic predictions of Jesus are meaningless and His words can be ignored. Christian politicians, journalists, theologians and preachers who are seeking to limit Jewish return to their own city are defying their faith. We are not saying that every action of the Jewish government, police or army is perfect. Nor is every action of any government perfect.

The unbelieving international community is extremely ignorant when they defy and ignore the plan of God. They think that through this they will bring peace. The opposite is true. "They have healed the wound of my people lightly, saying, 'Peace, peace,' when there is no peace." (Jer. 8:11) By ignoring God's clear plan to bring world peace and redemption they are setting the stage for international instability. All Christians believe that the return of Messiah Jesus will bring peace to this strife torn world

Only the Bible can predict events like this with such astonishing accuracy. The Bible is completely unlike any other book. God authenticates the accuracy of His word and His sovereignty over history and the outlines of His plan by describing events before they happen. Jesus gave the date of 1967 –1,934 years before the reunification of Jerusalem. Daniel spoke of Alexander more than 200 years before his conquest of the Middle East happened. God's word is truth. We are foolish when we ignore Him and His word. Our society ignores God's word thinking its plans and wisdom are better. God has a solution to our problems but we must listen to Him and not oppose His plans.

APPENDIX III

CHRONOLOGY OF THE BIBLE

4004 BC	Creation Of Adam
2348 BC	The Great Flood
1921 BC	Call & Covenant Of Abraham (430 Years Before The Exodus)
1896 BC	Isaac Born (Abraham 100)
1891 BC	Isaac Confirmed As Heir (400 Years Before The Exodus)
1836 BC	Jacob's Birth
1706 BC	Jacob's & Family Move to Egypt
1491 BC	Exodus (Exactly as God foretold in Gen. 12)
1451 BC	Joshua & Children Of Israel Enter The Land Of Promise
1055 BC	David Conquers Jerusalem
1015 BC	Solomon Begins His Reign
975 BC	Israel Divided Into Israel & Judah
721 BC	Northern Tribes Fall To Assyria
586 BC	Fall of Judah and Exile to Babylon
606-536	70 Years Exile To Babylon (Exactly as predicted in Jeremiah 29)
454 BC	Artaxerxes Decree To Rebuild Jerusalem (Start of 490 yr. Prophecy)

THE BLESSED HOPE

334 BC	Alexander Conquers Middle East
4 BC	Birth Of Jesus
32 AD	Death, & Resurrection Of Jesus (Exactly in the last 7 years of the 490 Years as predicted in Daniel 9)
70 AD	Fall Of Jerusalem To The Romans
637 AD	Jerusalem Conquered By Moslems
1099 - 1187	Crusader Christian Era
1250-1417	Egyptian Moslem Era Jerusalem
1417-1917	Jerusalem Under Ottoman Rule
1917-1948	Jerusalem Under British Mandate
1948 -1967	Jerusalem Under Jordanian Rule
1967 AD	Jerusalem Back To Jewish Control (2300 After Alexander's Conquest As Daniel & Jesus Foretold)

CURRENT & SOON EVENTS

- *Revival In Jerusalem (Zechariah 12)*

- *Opposition To Israel From The Nations (Zechariah 12) Islamic Powers*

- *Jerusalem To Be Divided By Nations (Zechariah 14)*

- *Jesus Returns To The Mt. Of Olives (Zech 14; Rev. 11:15)*

- *From Euphrates are defeated at Megiddo in Israel (Rev. 16)*

- *We Will Rise To Meet Him (2 Thess 4; Rev. 11:15)*

APPENDIX IV

THE IMPORTANCE OF BIBLE CHRONOLOGY

Chronology is one of the most interesting and awe-inspiring ways of studying the Bible. The Bible is like no other book and at vastly higher level than any other holy book or philosophical work. It is the only book that has accurate prophetic predictions of word events. In many cases the dates of specific events are given hundreds and even thousands of years before they happen.

This confirms the guiding hand of God, in and through and in spite of, all the chaotic events of History. It also confirms the inspiration and reliability of the word of God. It confirms that God is executing His plan and purpose in History, that history has a meaning and destiny and therefore our lives have meaning and purpose in His plan. It confirms God's faithfulness to His covenants and His promises to this day.

Of special interest to us are the three separations of Israel from its land and the prediction of the date of Jesus crucifixion. By

studying the chronology table above you can see that these prophecies were fulfilled precisely on the year foretold by the prophets.
- The 430-year period from the covenant of Israel and the Exodus prophesied by Abraham
    in Genesis 12
- The 40 year period between Isaac being declared heir and the Exodus (Genesis 15;13)
- The seventy-year exile prophesied by Jeremiah. (Jeremiah 29:10)
- The date of the Messiah's (first) coming and the completing of His ministry within 490
    years of a decree to restore and rebuild Jerusalem. (Daniel Chapter 9)
- And the prediction that Jerusalem would come back under Jewish control 2300 years after the conquest of the Middle East by a Greek King.

(This prophecy given by Daniel in Daniel Chapter 8 foretold the conquest of the Middle East by Alexander the Great 2000 years before Alexander's birth. It also foretells that 2300 years after Alexander's conquest Jerusalem would return to Jewish control. This prophecy was endorsed by Jesus (Luke 21:24) and fulfilled precisely in 1967. It confirms that the present day restoration of Israel and Jerusalem to Jewish control is no accident of history but is the pre-ordained fulfillment of the plan of God.

THE BLESSED HOPE

BIBLIOGRAPHY

"Islam In The End Of Times" by Ellis H. Skolfield
"The False Prophet" by Ellis H. Skolfield
"The Key To The Book Of Revelation" by David P
          Ebaugh
"The Rapture Plot" by Dave Macpherson
"The Incredible Cover Up" by David MacPherson
"God's Plan For Israel" by Stephen Kreloff
"Be Ye Ready" by Lance Lambert
"The Eternal Purposes of God" by Lance Lambert
"The Chronology Of The Old Testament" by Floyd Jones
"The Four Great Covenants" by Paul & Nuala O'Higgins

To order more copies Of **"The Blessed Hope"**
write to Reconciliation Outreach
P.O. Box 2778, Stuart, FL 34995
Or e-mail: paulandnuala@comcast.net
Or by going on line to
www.reconciliationoutreach.net

Books by Paul & Nuala O'Higgins
- Christianity Without Religion
- The Supernatural Habits
- Good News In Israel's Feasts
- The Four Great Covenants
- In Israel Today With Yeshua
- Have You Received The Holy Spirit?
- Life Changing World Changing Prayer.
- Time Of The Harvest
- Have You Received The Holy Spirit?
- The Real Mary
- Do This In Remembrance Of ME

ABOUT THE AUTHORS

Paul and Nuala O'Higgins are natives of Ireland who reside in Stuart Florida. They are the directors of Reconciliation Outreach – a ministry of teaching and interdenominational evangelism.

In full-time ministry together since 1977 they have ministered in over thirty nations. Nuala's degree is in education and Paul's degrees are in Philosophy and Theology. He holds a doctorate in Biblical Theology.

They are heralds of the love of God made available by the cross. Their call is to make known the treasures of God's kingdom and equip believers to be more effective followers of Jesus.

Made in the USA
Charleston, SC
25 September 2014